Editor
Eric Migliaccio

Managing Editor
Ina Massler Levin, M.A.

Editor-in-Chief
Sharon Coan, M.S. Ed.

Illustrator
Sue Fullam

Cover Artist
Brenda DiAntonis

Art Coordinator
Kevin Barnes

Imaging
Rosa C. See

Product Manager
Phil Garcia

Publisher
Mary D. Smith, M.S. Ed.

Correlations to the Common Core State Standards can be found at *http://www.teachercreated.com/ standards/*.

Nonfiction Reading Comprehension

Grade 4

Science · Geography · History

CORRELATED TO COMMON CORE STANDARDS

Teacher Created Resources

TCR 3384

W9-AJN-060

Author

Debra J. Housel, M.S. Ed.

Teacher Created Resources, Inc.
6421 Industry Way
Westminster, CA 92683
www.teachercreated.com

ISBN: 978-0-7439-3384-1

©2003 Teacher Created Resources, Inc.
Reprinted, 2013
Made in U.S.A.

The classroom teacher may reproduce copies of the materials in this book for use in a single classroom only. The reproduction of any part of the book for other classrooms or for an entire school or school system is strictly prohibited. No part of this publication may be transmitted, stored, or recorded in any form without written permission from the publisher.

Table of Contents

Introduction

Comprehension is the primary goal of any reading task. Students who comprehend expository text will have more opportunities in life, as well as better test performance. Through the use of nonfiction passages followed by exercises that require vital reading and thinking skills, *Nonfiction Reading Comprehension* will help you to develop confident readers and strengthen the comprehension skills necessary for a lifetime of learning.

Each passage in *Nonfiction Reading Comprehension* covers a grade-level appropriate curriculum topic in geography, history, and science. The activities are time-efficient, allowing students to practice these skills often. To yield the best results, such practice must begin during the second quarter, or when a solid majority of your class can read independently at a fourth-grade level.

✤ Essential Comprehension Skills

The questions following each passage in *Nonfiction Reading Comprehension* appear in the same order and cover seven vital skills:

✧ Locating facts

Questions based on exactly what the text states—who, what, when, where, why, and how many

✧ Identifying sequence

Questions based on chronological order—what happened first, last, and in between

✧ Noting conditions

Questions that ask students to identify similarities and differences, as well as cause-and-effect relationships

✧ Understanding vocabulary in context

Questions based on the ability to infer word meaning from the syntax and semantics of the surrounding text, as well as the ability to recognize known synonyms and antonyms for a newly encountered word

✧ Making inferences

Questions that require students to evaluate, to make decisions, and to draw logical conclusions

✧ Integrating knowledge

Questions that ask readers to draw upon their visualization skills combined with prior knowledge (These questions reinforce the crucial skill of picturing the text.)

✧ Supporting answers

A short-answer question at the end of each passage that helps students to personalize knowledge, state an opinion, and support it

Meeting Standards and Benchmarks

Every passage in *Nonfiction Reading Comprehension* and its comprehension questions cover one or more of these language arts standards:

Reading	Writing
• Makes and revises predictions about text	• Writes compound sentences
• Uses prior knowledge to understand new information presented in text	• Follows conventions of capitalization, spelling, and punctuation appropriate for grade level
• Visualizes what is read	• Uses adjectives, adverbs, and pronouns to make writing diverse and interesting
• Uses context clues to decode unknown words	• Adheres to grammatical and mechanical conventions in writing
• Monitors own reading and independently takes action to increase understanding (self-corrects, rereads, slows down if necessary)	• States an opinion and supports it in writing
• Understands the main idea of nonfiction text	
• Integrates new information into personal knowledge base	
• Draws conclusions and makes inferences about information in the text	
• Develops ideas, opinions, and personal responses to what is read	

The specific McREL content area standard and benchmark for each passage appears in a box at the top of each passage. Used with permission from McREL (Copyright 2000 McREL, Mid-continent Research for Education and Learning. Telephone: 303-337-0990. Web site: *www.mcrel.org*). Visit *http://www.teachercreated.com/standards/* for correlations to the Common Core State Standards.

✤ Readability

All of the passages have a 4.0–4.9 reading level based on the Flesch Kincaid Readability Formula. This formula, built into Microsoft Word, determines a readability level by calculating the number of words, syllables, and sentences. Although content area terms can be challenging, students can handle difficult words within the context given. The passages are presented in order of increasing difficulty within each content area.

✤ Preparing Students to Read Nonfiction Text

Each day, prepare your students to read the passages in *Nonfiction Reading Comprehension* by reading aloud a short nonfiction selection from another source. Reading expository text aloud is critical to developing your students' ability to read it themselves. Since making predictions is a good way to help students to understand nonfiction, read the beginning of a passage, then stop and ask them to predict what might occur next. Do this at several points throughout your reading of the text.

Talking about nonfiction concepts is also very important. Remember, however, that discussion can never replace reading aloud because people rarely speak using the vocabulary and complex sentence structures of written language.

How to Use This Book

If you have some students who cannot read the articles independently, allow them to read with a partner, then work through the comprehension questions alone. As soon as possible, move to having all students practice reading and answering the questions independently.

✢ Multiple-Choice Questions

Do the first two passages and related questions on pages 8–11 with the whole class. These passages have the most challenging reading level because you will do them together. Demonstrate your own cognitive process by thinking aloud about how to figure out an answer. This means that you essentially tell your students your thoughts as they come to you. Let's say that this is a passage your class has read:

> Years ago, 100,000 grizzly bears lived in the United States. Now there are only about 1,000, not including those that live in Alaska. In 1975 a law was passed to keep people from hunting the bears or destroying their homes. So today there are many more bears than in 1975. Almost all of them live in Yellowstone National Park. Sometimes the bears leave the park and kill cows or sheep. Some people feel afraid. They want to be able to shoot any grizzly that leaves the park. But others say that the bear population is already too small. They do not want the law changed.

Following the reading, one of the questions is: "In Yellowstone National park, grizzly bears a) live in cages, b) do tricks, c) get caught in traps, or d) wander around." Tell the students all your thoughts as they occur to you: "Well, the article said that the bears sometimes leave the park, so they must not be in cages. So I'll eliminate that choice. They are wild bears, so I doubt that they do any tricks. That leaves me with the choices 'get caught in traps' or 'wander around.' Let me look back at the article and see what it says about traps." Refer back to article. "I don't see anything about traps in the passage. And I did see that there is a law to keep the bears safe. That means they're safe from traps, which are dangerous. So I'm going to select '(d) wander around.'"

The fourth question is about vocabulary. Teach students to substitute each word choices for the vocabulary term (bolded) in the passage. For each substitution, they should ask, "Does this sentence make sense?" This will help them to identify the best choice.

Teach students to look for the key words in a response or question and search for those specific words in the text. Explain that they may need to look for synonyms for the key words. When you go over the practice passages, ask your students to show where they found the correct response in the text.

How to Use This Book (cont.)

✤ Short-Answer Questions

The short-answer question for each passage is an opinion statement with no definitive right answer. Each student makes a statement and explains it. While there is no correct response, it is critical to show them how to support their opinions using facts and logic. Show them a format for response: state their opinion followed by the word "because" and a reason. For example: "I do not think that whales should be kept at sea parks because they are wild animals. They want to be in the ocean with their friends." Do not award credit unless the student adequately supports his or her conclusion. Before passing back the practice papers, make note of two students with opposing opinions. Then, during the discussion, call on each of these students to read his or her short answer response to the class. If all your students drew the same conclusion or had the same opinion, come up with support for the opposing one yourself.

For the most effective practice sessions, follow these steps:

- Have students read the text silently and answer the questions.

- Collect all the papers to score them.

- Return the papers to the students and discuss how they determined their answers.

- Point out how students had to use their background knowledge to answer certain questions.

- Call on at least two students with different viewpoints to read and discuss their responses to the short-answer question.

- Have your students complete the achievement bar graph on page 7, showing how many questions they answered correctly for each practice passage. Seeing their scores improve or stay consistently high over time will provide encouragement and motivation.

Scoring the Passages

Since the passages are meant as skill builders, do not include the passage scores in students' class grades. With the students, use the "number correct" approach to scoring the practice passages, especially since this coincides with the student achievement graph on page 7. However, for your own records and to share with the parents, you may want to keep a track of numeric scores for each student. If you choose to do this, do not write the numeric score on the paper. To generate a numeric score, follow these guidelines:

Multiple Choice (6)	15 points each	90 points
Short Answer (1)	10 points	10 points
Total		**100 points**

✤ Practice Makes Perfect

The more your students practice, the more competent and confident they will become. Plan to have your class do every exercise in *Nonfiction Reading Comprehension*. If you do so, you'll be pleased with your students' improved comprehension of any expository text—within your classroom and beyond its walls.

Achievement Graph

Number Correct

Passage	1	2	3	4	5	6	7
"Trouble in the Coral Reefs"							
"Mount Rushmore"							
"Beaver Dams"							
"Light"							
"Water Is an Amazing Matter"							
"Your Remarkable Body"							
"Dandelions: Flowers or Food?"							
"May the Force Be With You"							
"The Orphan Trains"							
"A Most Unusual Fish"							
"A Highway in the Atlantic Ocean"							
"The Wonderful Walrus"							
"Blizzard!"							
"Looking for New Ways to Make Electricity"							
"Mummies in Ancient Egypt"							
"To Oregon or Bust!"							
"The Quaker Who Shook Things Up"							
"The Viking Ships"							
"The Generous Doctor"							
"The Pipes that Changed America"							

Geography Standard: Understands the characteristics of ecosystems on Earth's surface

Benchmark: Knows the components of ecosystems and how human intervention can change them

Trouble in the Coral Reefs

For millions of years, underwater ecosystems called coral reefs have provided homes and food for thousands of different living things. Fish and sea birds share the reef with giant clams, sea turtles, crabs, starfish, and many others. Now these beautiful places are in danger. So are all the sea plants and animals that depend on them. Scientists have found that people and pollution have ruined more than one-fourth of the Earth's coral reefs. Unless things change, all of the remaining reefs may die within your lifetime.

Some people think that coral is stone because of its rough, hard surface. But coral is an animal! Tiny polyps form the coral reefs. They come in many colors. These colors come from the algae living inside the coral. Billions of coral polyps stick together. New ones grow on the skeletons of dead coral. This happens year after year. Over time, the coral builds up a reef. The reef rises from the ocean floor until it almost reaches the sea's surface. It takes coral 500,000 years to build a huge reef. It has taken human beings less than 100 years to start wrecking the reefs.

The coral reefs have been harmed in different ways. People have broken off pieces of coral. They wanted to sell or keep them. To catch more fish, people have dropped sticks of **dynamite** into the water. This has blown up parts of reefs. Water pollution has encouraged overgrowth of the sea plants that grow near coral reefs. They block the sun that the algae need. The worst problem is the heating up of the world's oceans. Warm water kills the algae. When the algae dies, the coral loses both its food and its color. The coral turns white and dies. Scientists call this coral bleaching. The bleached part of the coral reef cannot recover.

Trouble in the Coral Reefs

Comprehension Questions

Fill in the bubble next to the best answer. You may look back at the story.

1. **Coral polyps are**

   (a) animals.

   (b) plants.

   (c) rocks.

   (d) algae.

2. **What happened first?**

   (a) The oceans got warmer.

   (b) The algae the coral needs died.

   (c) A coral reef formed.

   (d) Coral was bleached.

3. **Water pollution can cause problems for a coral reef because**

   (a) it makes a coral reef have many colors.

   (b) it can harm the coral.

   (c) it causes the coral skeletons to break down.

   (d) it makes the reef stick up out of the water.

4. **Another word for *dynamite* is**

   (a) clay.   (b) explosives.   (c) fire.   (d) poison.

5. **What will probably happen if all of the coral reefs die?**

   (a) Many ocean animals will die.

   (b) The ocean will get colder.

   (c) The ocean will get warmer.

   (d) The ocean will get deeper.

6. **Picture yourself swimming. You see red, yellow, and blue coral on a reef. Then you come to a part with white coral. Why is that part white?**

   (a) It is a more healthy part than the colored coral.

   (b) It is the newest part of the reef.

   (c) It is lava flowing in the sea.

   (d) It is a dead part of the reef.

7. **Do you think that it is important to save the coral reefs? Explain.**

   _____

   _____

   _____

History Standard: Understands the historical perspective

Benchmark: Understands that specific individuals had a great impact on history

Mount Rushmore

Each year many people go to see Mount Rushmore. This cliff in South Dakota has four men's heads carved into its rock. Each head is 60 feet (20 m) tall! It took workers 14 years to form them. They had to drill, chip, and blast to shape the hard rock into faces. The work was hard, but the men wore ropes to keep them safe. Once they began the second head, it started to crumble. They blasted it away. Then they carved it in a new spot. All of the rocks they chipped away lie in a big pile under the heads.

The heads are of George Washington, Thomas Jefferson, Theodore Roosevelt, and Abraham Lincoln. All of these men were U.S. presidents. Mount Rushmore honors these great leaders. What made them great? Each man did something important for the American people.

George Washington led the Revolutionary War. After it, our country was free to make its own laws. Then he led America for eight years as its first president.

Thomas Jefferson was our third president. He wrote the Declaration of Independence. This **document** told Britain that Americans would rule themselves. He later doubled the size of the U.S. by buying a lot of land west of the Mississippi River.

In the 1860s the states in the South wanted to form their own nation. Although it caused a war, Abraham Lincoln kept America united. He also set all of the slaves free in 1863. During a speech he said that all people were equal. No longer could one person own another.

Theodore Roosevelt started building the Panama Canal. This let ships go between the Atlantic and Pacific Oceans. This let cargo move faster and opened up trade. He also made sure that beautiful parts of the U.S. became national parks. This way everyone could enjoy them. If he had not done this, a rich person could have owned the Grand Canyon. Then other people could not have gone there. Mt. Rushmore is one of our national parks.

Mount Rushmore

Comprehension Questions

Fill in the bubble next to the best answer. You may look back at the story.

1. **Where is Mount Rushmore located?**

   (a) Washington, D.C.   (c) North Dakota

   (b) South Dakota   (d) Panama

2. **What happened last?**

   (a) The second head crumbled.

   (b) The men worked for 14 years.

   (c) People came from all over to see the mountain.

   (d) The four men on the mountain were presidents.

3. **Why did the second head probably start to crumble?**

   (a) A bomb hit it.

   (b) There was an earthquake.

   (c) It was struck by lightning.

   (d) There were already cracks in the rock it was carved in.

4. **A *document* is**

   (a) an official paper.

   (b) word processing.

   (c) a computer function.

   (d) a file folder.

5. **Look at the drawing of Mount Rushmore. You'll see that the men aren't carved in the order in which they served as president. Why do you think this is?**

   (a) The builders put the faces in order of the presidents' popularity.

   (b) The builders put each face where it best matched the natural rock face.

   (c) The builders didn't know the order in which the men served as president.

   (d) The builders weren't told whose faces that they were carving until they were almost done.

6. **Picture the men making Mount Rushmore. These men must not have been afraid of**

   (a) snakes.   (b) spiders.   (c) water.   (d) heights.

7. **If they were to add another president to Mount Rushmore, whom do you think they should add? Explain.**

   _____

   _____

   _____

Science Standard: Understands how species depend on one another and on the environment for survival

Benchmark: Knows that all organisms (including humans) cause changes in their environments, and these changes can be beneficial or detrimental

Beaver Dams

You hear and read about how people have changed the natural environment. But all animals and plants change their environments. One animal that makes big changes to its surroundings is the beaver. Beavers live in streams near wooded areas in North America, Europe, and Asia.

Beavers are large rodents with big, flat tails. They swim fast and can stay underwater for 15 minutes. While underwater, their ears and nostrils close. **Transparent** eyelids cover their eyes. This lets them see underwater.

Beavers make ponds from streams. They do this by building dams in the streams. Water backs up behind the dams, making ponds. Some water continues to flow through, so the streams are not totally gone.

To build their lodges, beavers first find deep, narrow spots in the ponds they have made. Then they cut down small trees using their sharp teeth. (Beavers' teeth grow every day, so they don't have to worry about wearing them down.) Next, they drag the logs to the ponds and "glue" them together with mud. The lodges always have two openings—both underwater. Beavers spend most of their time in their lodges. They cannot move fast on land. That makes it easy for wolves, bears, and bobcats to catch them. Beavers feel safer in the water.

The water in the ponds must be deep enough so that it won't freeze in winter. If it did, the entrances to the lodges would get blocked. Beavers do not hibernate during the winter. They come out of their lodges occasionally to eat tree bark, roots, and twigs. During warm weather they eat leaves and cattails, too.

Is it good that beavers turn streams into ponds? That depends on the kind of animal you are. If you are one that needs streams, like brook trout, you don't like it. However, the ponds gives homes to turtles, frogs, herons, and many more creatures.

Beaver Dams

Comprehension Questions

Fill in the bubble next to the best answer. You may look back at the story.

1. **Beavers build their lodges out of**
   - (a) clay.
   - (b) wood and mud.
   - (c) cattails and clay.
   - (d) wood and glue.

2. **What happens first?**
   - (a) A beaver builds a dams.
   - (b) The beaver chews down trees.
   - (c) A pond forms behind the dam.
   - (d) A beaver finds a good spot in a stream.

3. **When are beavers in the most danger?**
   - (a) while they are swimming
   - (b) while they are on shore
   - (c) inside their lodge
   - (d) while climbing trees

4. **If something is *transparent*, it means you can**
   - (a) not use it.
   - (b) use it.
   - (c) not see through it.
   - (d) see through it.

5. **Which animal is a rodent?**
   - (a) a cat
   - (b) a fox
   - (c) a rat
   - (d) a pig

6. **Picture the shore near a beaver lodge. What do you see there?**
   - (a) tree stumps
   - (b) a waterfall
   - (c) a sandy beach
   - (d) a skyscraper

7. **Would you like to see the inside of a beaver's lodge? Explain.**

   _____

   _____

   _____

Science Standard: Understands motion and the principles that explain it

Benchmark: Knows ways in which light interacts with matter (including refraction, absorption, scattering, and reflection)

Light

Light is a form of energy. Without it we could see nothing. A ray of white light contains all of the colors of the rainbow. It travels in a straight line from its source. If something opaque (such as a box) gets into the light's path, the light bounces off its surface. It scatters, or spreads out. The light beams cannot go through the object, so opaque things cast well-defined shadows. We can see opaque things the most easily. For example, grass looks green because it scatters green light from its surface. The grass absorbs the other colors of white light. The colors black and white do not follow this rule. Black absorbs all of the colors of white light. That's why it looks black. White absorbs none of the colors of white light, which is why it looks white.

You can see through transparent objects. They let all light rays pass through them. They cast no shadow. Air, water, and glass are all transparent. However, water and glass are not completely transparent. That's why we can't see air, but we can see water and glass. Translucent objects, such as a cloud or a lampshade, let some light through. They cut down the light's glare and cast fuzzy shadows. Light does not travel as quickly through translucent objects as it does through transparent ones.

Another interesting quality of light is refraction. When you put a drinking straw into a clear glass of water, the straw appears to bend beneath the water's surface. You know that the straw is really still straight. The bend you see comes from refraction. The way that light travels through transparent items causes refraction. Since air particles are far apart, air is not dense. Light can move the most rapidly through air. Water is a liquid because its particles are closer together. Because it's denser, it slows the light down. Glass is the most dense of the three. As a solid, the particles in glass are very close together. Light must slow down as it moves through these dense particles. This makes the ray of light bend, which causes the **illusion** of the bent straw.

A mirror only works when light hits it. A mirror is anything with such a smooth surface that it can reflect images. Most often a mirror is a piece of glass with a silver backing, but it can also be a clear, still body of water or a piece of shiny metal. So how does your bathroom mirror reflect? A ray of light shines through the glass in the front. It reaches the shiny silver and bounces back through the glass.

Light

Comprehension Questions

Fill in the bubble next to the best answer. You may look back at the story.

1. The color black absorbs

(a) one of the colors of white light.

(b) the dark colors of white light.

(c) none of the colors of white light.

(d) all of the colors of white light.

2. What happens last?

(a) The ray of light travels in a straight line.

(b) You turn on a light in a dark room.

(c) The chair casts a shadow.

(d) The ray of light hits a chair.

3. You look into the mirror in your bathroom, but you can't see yourself. Why?

(a) The mirror is too old to reflect.

(b) There isn't enough light for the mirror to reflect.

(c) The mirror is cracked.

(d) The mirror is hanging crooked on the wall.

4. *Illusion* means

(a) something is not really the way that it looks.

(b) something that looks like clear glass.

(c) fabric you can see through.

(d) something that looks fancy.

5. What are sheer curtains?

(a) transparent

(b) translucent

(c) opaque

(d) invisible

6. Picture a tree on a sunny day. Now picture it on an overcast day when you can't see the sun. What's different on the overcast day?

(a) The tree is dry.

(b) The tree is a different color.

(c) The tree doesn't cast a shadow.

(d) The tree's leaves are drooping.

7. One dark night the power goes off at your house. Would you rather have a candle or a flashlight? Explain.

_____

_____

_____

Science Standard: Understands basic concepts about the structure and properties of matter

Benchmark: Knows that materials have different states (solid, liquid, and gas) and some common materials such as water can be changed from one state to another by heating or cooling

Water Is an Amazing Matter

Everything consists of matter. Matter is any **substance** that has weight and takes up space. Matter can be a liquid, a solid, or a gas.

Water can be found in all three forms. When water is a liquid, we drink it or take a shower. When water is a solid, we put cubes of it into a drink to keep it cool. We like to sled, ski, or skate on solid water. When water is a gas, we call it water vapor. When water boils, at least some of it changes into a gas. When a teakettle whistles, steam—which is water vapor—comes out of it.

Water vapor also evaporates from the ground. This happens when the sun shines after it rains. The water vapor collects into clouds. The wind blows the clouds around. With the right conditions, the cloud vapor turns back into liquid. Then it falls to the ground as rain, snow, hail, or sleet.

What makes water change its form? It all depends on the water's temperature. When water is cold—0°C or 32°F or less—it is a solid, such as ice or snow. When water is warmer, it is a liquid. When water boils—at 100°C or 212°F or more—it becomes vapor. Some people think that the amount of water changes when the water moves from one state to another. They believe that some of the water gets lost during the change. Actually the amount of water always stays the same, no matter which state the water is in. People are tricked due to the amount of space the water uses in its different forms. Solid ice takes up more space than liquid. Water vapor takes up the least amount of space.

Water Is an Amazing Matter

Comprehension Questions

Fill in the bubble next to the best answer. You may look back at the story.

1. **When water boils it becomes**
   ⓐ a liquid.
   ⓑ a solid.
   ⓒ a vapor.
   ⓓ another substance.

2. **Think about the water cycle. Starting with water in a lake, which of the following happens last?**
   ⓐ Snow falls.
   ⓑ Water vapor rises into the atmosphere.
   ⓒ The water vapor turns into snow.
   ⓓ Water vapor collects into clouds.

3. **What happens when you add ice cubes to a drink?**
   ⓐ The ice cubes make the drink bubbly.
   ⓑ The ice cubes melt.
   ⓒ The drink heats up.
   ⓓ As the ice cubes melt, the drink overflows the glass.

4. ***Substance* means**
   ⓐ object.   ⓒ material.
   ⓑ liquid.   ⓓ solid.

5. **A glacier is water in what form?**
   ⓐ solid   ⓒ liquid
   ⓑ gas   ⓓ vapor

6. **Picture looking into a pot of boiling water. How can you tell that the water is boiling?**
   ⓐ The water smells different.
   ⓑ The water has turned solid.
   ⓒ The water has changed color.
   ⓓ The water is bubbling.

7. **What food do you like that you must boil water in order to make? Explain.**

   _____

   _____

   _____

Science Standard: Knows the general structure and functions of cells in organisms

Benchmark: Knows that each plant or animal has different structures which serve different functions in growth, survival, and reproduction

Your Remarkable Body

Your body is an amazing machine. A machine has many parts that work together to make it run. In much the same way, a human has body systems that work together to keep a person going. One system is not more important than another. All are necessary in order for the body to live. Two of these systems include the circulatory system and the **respiratory** system.

The circulatory system moves blood throughout the body. Your cells need a constant supply of fresh blood. Blood has red blood cells, white blood cells, and platelets. The red blood cells carry oxygen from the lungs to the rest of the body. They also bring back carbon dioxide and waste. White blood cells attack germs to keep the body healthy. Platelets stop bleeding by forming a clot. Without platelets, you could bleed to death from a small cut!

Your heart is about the size of your fist. This muscle pumps blood through blood vessels. Actually the heart has two pumps. The heart's left pump gets blood from the lungs. This blood has oxygen. The heart pumps it to cells all over the body. The heart's right pump gets the blood returning from the cells. This blood has carbon dioxide in it. The right pump moves this blood to the lungs. There the carbon dioxide is taken out of the blood, and oxygen is added.

As you can see, the respiratory system gives the body oxygen and gets rid of carbon dioxide. When you inhale, your lungs get bigger. Oxygen rushes into them. When you exhale, your chest gets smaller, pushing carbon dioxide out. Air enters through the nose or mouth. Inside your nose are millions of tiny hairs. These hairs trap dust and dirt so that only clean air goes down the trachea, or windpipe, to the lungs. Right above the lungs, the windpipe splits into two tubes. One tube enters each lung. Inside the lungs these tubes branch into many smaller tubes. These smaller tubes have millions of air sacs. Carbon dioxide and oxygen are exchanged in these air sacs. Carbon dioxide leaves the blood and goes into the air sacs. Then oxygen moves through the air sacs into the blood. This oxygen-filled blood goes to the heart. The carbon dioxide leaves the lungs with the next exhale.

Your Remarkable Body

Comprehension Questions

Fill in the bubble next to the best answer. You may look back at the story.

1. **How many air sacs are in your lungs?**
   - ⓐ dozens
   - ⓑ hundreds
   - ⓒ thousands
   - ⓓ millions

2. **What happens last?**
   - ⓐ John cuts his knee.
   - ⓑ The platelets in his blood rush to the cut.
   - ⓒ John's knee stops bleeding.
   - ⓓ John's knee bleeds.

3. **Which is true?**
   - ⓐ The air around us has only oxygen in it.
   - ⓑ We use all of the elements in the air that we breathe.
   - ⓒ We breathe in oxygen and exhale carbon dioxide.
   - ⓓ We breathe in carbon dioxide and exhale oxygen.

4. **The word *respiratory* means**
   - ⓐ eating.
   - ⓑ pumping.
   - ⓒ smelling.
   - ⓓ breathing.

5. **When someone is choking, something is blocking their**
   - ⓐ trachea.
   - ⓑ platelets.
   - ⓒ heart.
   - ⓓ veins.

6. **Picture a person with a deep cut on her leg. Which body system is affected?**
   - ⓐ digestive
   - ⓑ circulatory
   - ⓒ skeleton
   - ⓓ respiratory

7. **What part of your body do you consider the most amazing? Explain.**

   _____

   _____

   _____

Science Standard: Knows about the diversity and unity that characterize life

Benchmark: Knows that plants and animals progress through life cycles; the details of these life cycles are different for different organisms

Dandelions: Flowers or Food?

Hundreds of years ago no dandelions grew in North America. Then people came from Europe. They had dandelion seeds on their clothes. The seeds fell from their clothes onto the ground. Since then dandelions have spread all over.

Most people believe that dandelions are weeds. They do not want them in their yards. But some people think that dandelion flowers are pretty. And others think that dandelions taste good. They cook dandelion leaves or put them into a fresh salad. The leaves must be picked before the flowers bloom or they will not taste good. Some people make dandelion flowers into wine.

Dandelions do not die easily. During a mild winter, their leaves may stay green. When the spring comes, they **blossom**. Each night their bright yellow flowers close up. When the sun shines the next day, they open up again. Dandelion flowers are very unusual. They do not have to get pollen from another dandelion flower in order to form seeds. So after several days, the yellow flower turns white and puffy. A tiny brown seed forms at the bottom of each white petal. When the wind blows, the petals float away. Each white petal acts like a parachute, carrying a seed away. This lets the dandelions spread their seeds all over. New dandelions grow where the seeds land.

Dandelions: Flowers or Food?

Comprehension Questions

Fill in the bubble next to the best answer. You may look back at the story.

1. Dandelions are

(a) flowers. (c) food.

(b) weeds. (d) all of the above

2. What happens last in the life cycle of a dandelion?

(a) The dandelions grow yellow flowers.

(b) The seeds blow away.

(c) Seeds form at the base of the white petals.

(d) The petals turn white.

3. When is the best time to pick dandelion leaves to eat?

(a) before the flowers bloom

(b) after the flowers bloom

(c) in the winter

(d) after dark

4. Another word for *blossom* is

(a) grow. (c) bloom.

(b) seed. (d) form.

5. New dandelions

(a) can be far away from the parent dandelion.

(b) must grow near the parent dandelion.

(c) come up from the roots of a dandelion.

(d) are bigger than the parent dandelion.

6. Picture the dandelion seeds first coming to North America on a woman's clothing. What is she wearing?

(a) jeans and a T-shirt

(b) a business suit

(c) a long dress

(d) a pair of shorts and a tank top

7. If you had a garden, what kinds of things would you grow? Explain.

_____

_____

_____

Science Standard: Understands motion and the principles that explain it

Benchmark: Knows that when a force is applied to an object, the object either speeds up, slows down, or goes in a different direction

May the Force Be With You

A force is anything that pushes or pulls to make an object move. Our world has natural forces. Sir Isaac Newton said that all matter has inertia. *Inertia* means that any object stays still or moves in the same way until a force acts upon it. For example, a cup placed on a table will stay there until someone or something creates a force to move it. Inertia also means that an ice skate will stay gliding across ice in a straight path until the person wearing it changes direction, falls, or runs out of ice.

Gravity, which pulls everything towards the ground, is one force. Another is *magnetic force*. Magnets can pull metal objects closer together or push them further apart. *Friction* is an important force, too. Friction works to slow or stop movement between any two surfaces that rub together. Without friction, a person couldn't run; and once that person was moving, he or she couldn't stop. A person couldn't pick up or kick a ball because it would slip away. Hikers wear boots with deep tread to increase friction. Baseball and football players wear cleats for the same reason. A soccer goalie wears gloves to make it easier to catch and hold the ball.

A lack of friction lets things slide. Any smooth surface, such as a kitchen counter, has less friction than a rough surface, such as a brick. Sometimes a lack of friction is good; other times it's bad. Snow has little friction. This lets skiers glide across it. Bikers oil their gears to make the wheels spin faster. Wet pavement also has little friction. This may cause a car to slide off the road or into another car.

Drag is a similar force. Drag is the force of air or water slowing down the things that move through them. Engineers design jets and cars to be **aerodynamic** to reduce drag. Then the object slices through the air, letting it move faster. To cut down on the drag in water, swimmers wear caps. This lets them glide through the water more rapidly. Fish have sleek bodies that can move efficiently through water. People design racing boats to do the same thing.

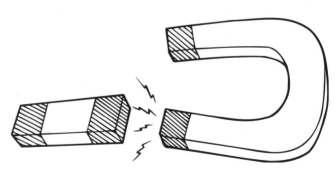

May the Force Be With You

Comprehension Questions

Fill in the bubble next to the best answer. You may look back at the story.

1. **What force makes something that you drop fall?**
   - (a) magnetic
   - (b) gravity
   - (c) friction
   - (d) drag

2. **What happens last?**
   - (a) The ball rolls.
   - (b) You kick a ball in a field.
   - (c) The ground's friction makes the ball stop.
   - (d) Inertia keeps the ball going.

3. **Who wants to decrease the force of friction?**
   - (a) a sledder
   - (b) a soccer player
   - (c) a mountain climber
   - (d) a race car driver

4. **Something that is *aerodynamic***
   - (a) flies high.
   - (b) cannot crash.
   - (c) looks modern.
   - (d) glides through air without difficulty.

5. **Who relies on the force of drag?**
   - (a) a weightlifter
   - (b) a runner
   - (c) a person in a parachute
   - (d) a person playing a flute

6. **Picture an ice hockey player hitting a puck towards a goal. If no one stops the puck, it will score a goal because of the force called**
   - (a) inertia.
   - (b) drag.
   - (c) gravity.
   - (d) friction.

7. **Name your favorite sport. Explain how a natural force affects the sport.**

   _____

   _____

   _____

Geography Standard: Understands the nature, distribution, and migration of human populations on Earth's surface

Benchmark: Understands voluntary and involuntary migration

The Orphan Trains

In the late 1800s and early 1900s there were a great many orphans in New York City. An orphan is a child whose parents are dead. Thousands of **destitute** children lived in the streets. They slept in old boxes or under bridges. They begged or stole food. Some of these children were only two years old.

Nuns started orphanages—places where these children could sleep in a bed and eat a little food. But there were many more children than they could help. Charles Loring Brace believed that all of the children needed homes and families, not just beds and food. In 1854 he came up with an idea to help both the children and the families who took them in. He decided to send the children out west. There, farm families could adopt the children. Farmers could usually feed another person. Many could use another pair of hands to help with the chores.

The first group of children was told what was happening. A few of these children did not want to go. They felt afraid. They did not want new families. They believed that a relative would come and get them. They tried to jump off the train. After that the children were told only that they were going on a train ride. They each wore new outfits so that they would look their best.

During the next 75 years about 200,000 children rode these trains. A poster in each town on the railroad told people when the children would arrive. When the train pulled in, the children lined up on the station platform. The people who wanted a child would pick one. The children who were not chosen got back on the train and went to the next town. Often brothers and sisters got separated this way. Some of the children never felt like they belonged in the new family. But most of the children found parents who cared about them. They found love and a new life by riding the orphan train.

The Orphan Trains

Comprehension Questions

Fill in the bubble next to the best answer. You may look back at the story.

1. **About how many children went west on orphan trains?**
   - (a) 200
   - (b) 2,000
   - (c) 20,000
   - (d) 200,000

2. **What happened first?**
   - (a) A child's parents died.
   - (b) The child was given a new outfit.
   - (c) The child lived on the streets.
   - (d) The child rode an orphan train.

3. **Whose life today is similar to those orphans of long ago?**
   - (a) movie stars
   - (b) railroad engineers
   - (c) homeless people
   - (d) children in hospitals

4. **People who are *destitute* are**
   - (a) so poor that they have nowhere to live.
   - (b) so bad that they have gone to jail.
   - (c) so ill that they will probably die.
   - (d) so crippled that they cannot move.

5. **How did the children probably feel when they were separated from their brothers and sisters?**
   - (a) excited
   - (b) sleepy
   - (c) glad
   - (d) upset

6. **Picture a nun searching for orphans in New York City. Where is she looking?**
   - (a) in homes
   - (b) under bridges
   - (c) in tents
   - (d) in restaurants

7. **If you had been one of the orphans, would you have wanted to go on the orphan train?**

   _____

   _____

   _____

Geography Standard: Understands the characteristics of ecosystems on Earth's surface

Benchmark: Knows plants and animals associated with various vegetation and climatic regions on Earth

A Most Unusual Fish

What has a tail like a monkey, a head like a horse, and a pouch like a kangaroo? It's the small, odd fish called a sea horse. Sea horses have long, flexible tails that they use to cling to sea plants. They use their long snouts to suck up and eat plankton. Plankton are animals too tiny for us to see without a **microscope**.

Sea horses reproduce in an unusual way. The male has a pouch. The female lays up to 100 eggs in his pouch. The male carries the eggs around for six weeks. Then he labors to give birth to tiny, live babies. The babies hold each other's tails until they float to the safety of a patch of seaweed or a coral reef. Then they let go of each other and go their separate ways.

If they can avoid predators, the babies can live to be three years old. Since a sea horse must move through the water in an upright position, it cannot swim well. This means that it can't rely on speed to escape from predators. Many animals that try to eat a sea horse will spit it out. Why? Sea horses have bony knobs and spines covering their body. Sharks, sea turtles, barracudas, and stingrays will eat them, anyway. So sea horses cling to coral reefs. They blend in by changing color to match their surroundings.

Sea horses must live in warm salt water. How big they grow depends on where they live. The biggest sea horses live off the coast of California, Australia, and New Zealand. Smaller ones can be found near Florida, in the Gulf of Mexico, and the Caribbean Sea.

A Most Unusual Fish

Comprehension Questions

Fill in the bubble next to the best answer. You may look back at the story.

1. Sea horses live in
   (a) cold lakes.
   (b) warm lakes.
   (c) cold parts of oceans.
   (d) warm parts of oceans.

2. What happened first?
   (a) The sea horse babies float away.
   (b) The female puts eggs into the male's pouch.
   (c) Tiny baby sea horses are born.
   (d) The male carries the eggs for weeks.

3. Why do sea horses change color?
   (a) to hide from enemies
   (b) to attract a mate
   (c) to lure plankton closer
   (d) to find a home

4. A *microscope* makes things appear
   (a) brighter.
   (b) darker.
   (c) bigger.
   (d) smaller.

5. A predator grabs a sea horse in its mouth. Instead of eating it, the predator spits it out because
   (a) the sea horse bit the predator.
   (b) the predator wasn't really hungry.
   (c) the predator didn't like how the sea horse tasted.
   (d) the predator didn't like the sea horse's bony outer covering.

6. You are scuba diving at a coral reef. You see many sea horses. What else do you see in the water?
   (a) tropical fish
   (b) walruses
   (c) seals
   (d) penguins

7. In some places sea horses are endangered. Should we work to protect sea horses?

_____

_____

_____

Geography Standard: Understands how physical systems affect human systems

Benchmark: Knows the ways in which human activities are constrained by the physical environment

A Highway in the Atlantic Ocean

Did you know that a river runs in the Atlantic Ocean? Actually, it's a long, powerful ocean current called the Gulf Stream. Its water flows along the coasts of North America and Europe.

The ocean has many currents. Some currents flow east to west. Others go south to north. Still others move up and down between the surface and the depths. The Gulf Stream is a wide river of warm water. It comes from the Equator and heads north.

Flowing about 4 miles per hour (6.5 kph), it follows the East Coast of the U.S. Near Cape Cod, Massachusetts, the current turns to the right and crosses the ocean. Then it splits. Some of the water goes south past Spain and Africa. The rest of the water flows along the coast of Great Britain and Ireland. The Gulf Stream's warm water heats the air above it. Parts of Ireland are so warm that palm trees grow. Great Britain gets a much milder winter than Newfoundland, Canada, even though both places are the same distance north of the Equator.

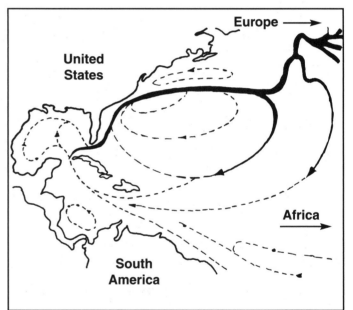

About 500 years ago, ship captains used the Gulf Stream as a "sea highway" to make their ocean **voyages** shorter. They knew that they would move faster if they sailed from America to Europe with the current. They could cover up to 75 more miles per day. On the trip from Europe to America, if they sailed against the current they could be slowed down so much that they would arrive two weeks later than planned!

People wanted to know more about the current. Out at sea, sailors dropped glass bottles with notes inside. The notes said when and where they were dropped. Where the bottles were found on shore told about the water's direction and speed. Today people still study the Gulf Stream. Now they know that some of the water at the edge drifts away. Later it returns to the main current, forming a big circle. Recently people learned that another current runs in the opposite direction deep below the Gulf Stream.

A Highway in the Atlantic Ocean

Comprehension Questions

Fill in the bubble next to the best answer. You may look back at the story.

1. **How long have people known there is a Gulf Stream?**
   - ⓐ at least 500 years
   - ⓑ for about 50 years
   - ⓒ it has just been discovered in the last few years
   - ⓓ 10,000 years

2. **What happens first?**
   - ⓐ The Gulf Stream flows across the ocean.
   - ⓑ The Gulf Stream flows north from the equator.
   - ⓒ The Gulf Stream splits with some water flowing north and the rest going south.
   - ⓓ The Gulf Stream goes along the East Coast of the United States.

3. **Why did a ship's captain need to know about the Gulf Stream?**
   - ⓐ so he could always avoid it
   - ⓑ so he wouldn't get shipwrecked
   - ⓒ so he could avoid dangerous currents
   - ⓓ so he could use it to travel faster

4. ***Voyages* means**
   - ⓐ waves.
   - ⓑ adventures.
   - ⓒ journeys.
   - ⓓ problems.

5. **If the Gulf Stream changed where it flowed, how would the Earth be affected?**
   - ⓐ It would cause severe thunderstorms.
   - ⓑ There would be huge undersea earthquakes.
   - ⓒ There would be big volcanic eruptions.
   - ⓓ The climate would change in several places.

6. **Picture palm trees growing in Ireland. Why do they look out of place?**
   - ⓐ because usually only pine trees grow in Ireland
   - ⓑ because palm trees usually only grow in the tropics
   - ⓒ because Ireland is so small
   - ⓓ because Ireland has no summer

7. **Should we continue to study the Gulf Stream? Explain.**

   _____

   _____

   _____

Geography Standard: Understands the characteristics of ecosystems on Earth's surface

Benchmark: Knows plants and animals associated with various vegetation and climatic regions on Earth

The Wonderful Walrus

Walruses are large sea mammals that live in the Arctic Ocean, where the water is always cold. They have flippers and a tail, which they use to swim at speeds up to 20 miles per hour (32 kph).

Walruses eat clams that live on the ocean floor. They dive deep to get the clams. The sunlight cannot reach that far, and it is pitch black. So walruses have whiskers called *vibrissae*. These special whiskers can feel things. When its vibrissae indicate that clams are nearby, the walrus fills its mouth with water and squirts it at the clams. This powerful burst of water pushes away the sand from the clams so the walrus can eat them.

Walruses have tusks made of ivory, just like those of elephants. Walruses use these tusks in many ways. When they come to the water's surface, they want to warm up by lying on a floating piece of ice. Walruses can weigh half a ton, yet these **massive** animals get out of the water and onto the ice with grace and ease. How? They plant their tusks in the ice, just like a mountain climber uses an ice ax. Then they use their strong neck muscles to pull themselves out of the water.

The walrus with the longest tusks is the most important one in a group. That's because walruses use their tusks as weapons, too. They live in big groups, and sometimes they fight. The walrus with the biggest tusks wins. They also use their tusks to ward off polar bears. In fact, polar bears always avoid adult walruses because of their sharp tusks.

Years ago, people used to kill walruses for their tusks. They wanted to carve the ivory into tools, statues, or decorations. Now it is illegal to hunt for walruses.

The Wonderful Walrus

Comprehension Questions

Fill in the bubble next to the best answer. You may look back at the story.

1. What do walruses eat?

  (a) each other   (c) polar bears

  (b) clams   (d) vibrissae

2. What happens first?

  (a) The walrus dives to the ocean floor.

  (b) The walrus eats.

  (c) The walrus uses its vibrissae.

  (d) The walrus squirts water at a clam.

3. Why did people used to hunt walruses?

  (a) for their vibrissae

  (b) for their blubber

  (c) for their ivory

  (d) for their fur

4. Another word for *massive* is

  (a) lazy.   (c) ugly.

  (b) huge.   (d) weak.

5. The most important walruses are the ones who

  (a) have the shortest vibrissae.

  (b) fight polar bears.

  (c) have the biggest tusks.

  (d) have help getting up onto the ice.

6. Picture a group of walruses on the ice. A polar bear is moving closer. Which walrus does the polar bear try to grab?

  (a) the closest walrus

  (b) the one with the biggest tusks

  (c) the one with the worst whiskers

  (d) a baby at the edge of the group

7. Which do you like better: walruses or polar bears? Explain.

_____

_____

_____

Geography Standard: Understands how physical systems affect human systems

Benchmark: Knows natural hazards that occur in the physical environment

Blizzard!

A blizzard is more than just a bad snowstorm. It's a powerful snowstorm with strong, cold winds. Blizzards usually come after a spell of warm winter weather. A mass of cold air moves down from the Arctic Circle. This cold, heavy air drops down while the warmer, moist air rises. This forms a cold front. The result is a heavy snowfall whipped by bitter north winds.

The National Weather Service of the United States defines a blizzard as a snowstorm with winds of 35 miles per hour (56 kph). The blowing snow makes it hard to see even a foot or two ahead. During a really severe blizzard, winds gust at over 45 miles per hour (72 kph). Then **visibility** is zero. Temperatures can drop to 10°F (-12°C).

A huge blizzard in March 1888 covered the eastern U.S., choking New York City. It took more than a week to dig the city out. During that time many people froze to death inside their homes. Blizzards caused trouble for the settlers in the West, too. The dangerous weather came without much warning. People had to rush to get themselves and their animals indoors. Otherwise they would die. Sometimes people were found frozen just a few feet away from their house or barn. They just couldn't see well enough to find shelter. It was risky to be out in a storm, yet someone had to feed the animals. So people tacked one end of a rope to their barn. They nailed the other end of the rope to their house. They went back and forth holding the rope. This kept them from getting lost in the blinding snow.

Blizzards happen in the U.S. Northern Plains states, in eastern and central Canada, and in parts of Russia. The high winds can blow snow into huge drifts 15 feet (5 m) high. These snowdrifts often stop all transportation. Schools and businesses close down for days until all of the snow gets cleared away. During that time, if a person needs to get to the hospital, an ambulance cannot help. Instead the person must go in a snowplow!

Blizzard!

Comprehension Questions

Fill in the bubble next to the best answer. You may look back at the story.

1. How does a blizzard differ from a regular snowstorm?
- (a) A blizzard has high winds that blow lots of snow around.
- (b) A blizzard has lots of snow but no wind.
- (c) A blizzard has high winds but no snow.
- (d) No one knows when a blizzard is coming.

2. What would happen first?
- (a) The ambulance sent a snowplow to help Ms. Ramirez.
- (b) Ms. Ramirez called an ambulance.
- (c) There was a blizzard.
- (d) Ms. Ramirez had a medical emergency.

3. Why does transportation usually halt during a blizzard?
- (a) The snowdrifts bury all vehicles.
- (b) Winds blow the vehicles right off the road.
- (c) It's too cold for any engine to run.
- (d) People can't see well enough to drive or to fly.

4. *Visibility* means
- (a) the ability to smell.
- (b) the ability to see.
- (c) the ability to hear.
- (d) the ability to feel.

5. Why do blizzards occur in the areas stated in the passage?
- (a) because these places are far from the Arctic Circle
- (b) because these places are near the Arctic Circle
- (c) because these places are south of the Equator
- (d) because these places are near Antarctica

6. Picture yourself watching the weather on TV. The weather forecaster says that a blizzard will hit your area tonight. You can expect that tomorrow you will most likely
- (a) have no light, heat, water, or phone service.
- (c) go to the grocery store for food.
- (b) go to school.
- (d) stay at home.

7. Do you think that modern weather forecasting has helped more people to survive blizzards? Explain.

_____

_____

_____

Geography Standard: Understands the changes that occur in the meaning, use, distribution, and importance of resources

Benchmark: Knows the characteristics, location, and use of renewable resources and nonrenewable resources

Looking for New Ways to Make Electricity

Think of how you used electricity today. Did you cook breakfast in the microwave? Did you turn on a light? Did you use a computer? All of these things used electrical power.

Electrical power must be made. Usually this means that a power plant burns gas, oil, or coal to generate electricity. But these are all fossil fuels. Just like fossils, these fuels formed deep underground over millions of years. Dead plants and animals rotted. After millions of years and lots of pressure from the weight of the ground above, they changed into gas, oil, or coal. The world has used fossil fuels for energy for more than 100 years. Burning them causes a lot of pollution. Also, the Earth is running out of fossil fuels. Within 40 years there probably won't be any left. And we certainly can't wait a million years for more to be made!

What will we do? Scientists are trying to figure that out. They want to find new ways to make electricity. They'd like the new ways not to cause pollution. They hope to find **renewable** energy sources. This means that, unlike fossil fuels, they can never run out. What could possibly meet those demands? The sun and the wind can.

Right now no one knows the best way to capture the sun's rays and turn them it into electrical power. Still, Japan and other countries have built some houses with solar roof tiles. The tiles collect sunshine even on overcast days. So far these tiles have worked so well that they have made all of the electricity the family needs each day. Some cars have already been built that use solar tiles for part of their power.

For hundreds of years people in the Netherlands used windmills for their energy. Today's windmills are taller and have lightweight blades to catch more wind. Some have propellers mounted on heads that can turn. This lets the windmill get the most wind possible, no matter which way the wind blows. In the driest parts of the western U.S., wind farms have sprung up. Hundreds of windmills stand on otherwise unused land. The electricity they generate powers homes and businesses in cities many miles away.

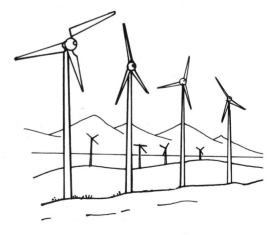

Looking for New Ways to Make Electricity

Comprehension Questions

Fill in the bubble next to the best answer. You may look back at the story.

1. Why do we need to find non-fossil fuel methods of making electricity?

ⓐ Fossil fuels don't work with modern engines.

ⓑ No one knows the best way to use fossil fuels.

ⓒ The world is running out of fossil fuels.

ⓓ Fossil fuels are too expensive to use.

2. What happens last?

ⓐ Layers of rocks and mud cover dead plants.

ⓑ People remove the fossil fuel from underground.

ⓒ The dead plants are under a lot of pressure.

ⓓ After a long time, the dead plants turn into gas, oil, or coal.

3. If we run out of fossil fuels, we will

ⓐ have to use another source of energy.

ⓑ have to find a cleaner source of water.

ⓒ make more fossil fuels.

ⓓ stop using electricity.

4. *Renewable* means

ⓐ computerized.   ⓒ inexpensive.

ⓑ abundant.   ⓓ able to be used repeatedly.

5. Which energy source is the best for our environment?

ⓐ oil   ⓒ sunshine

ⓑ coal   ⓓ trees

6. Visualize food cooking in a microwave. How is the oven getting power?

ⓐ from microwaves in the air

ⓑ from a wall outlet

ⓒ from the sun

ⓓ from the food being cooked inside of it

7. Which do you think is the best way to generate electricity? Explain.

_____

_____

_____

History Standard: Understands selected attributes and historical developments of societies in Africa, the Americas, Asia, and Europe

Benchmark: Knows significant historical achievements of various cultures of the world

Mummies in Ancient Egypt

Thousands of years ago people in Ancient Egypt thought that dead people needed their bodies after death. They believed that the people continued to live in a place called the afterlife. So they found a way to keep dead bodies from rotting. They figured out how to turn dead people into mummies. They **preserved** most of their kings and queens this way.

It was a lot of work to make a mummy. First, priests washed the dead body. Then they removed all of the organs—even the brain! They put a kind of salt all over the body. After six weeks, the body completely dried out. Next, they stuffed the body with sand, sawdust, or cloth. This made the body look full again. Then they rubbed spices and oils into the skin. Finally the priests wrapped cloth strips tightly around each part of the body. Wrapping the body took about two weeks. At last they put the body into a coffin. On its cover the coffin had paintings and sometimes gems.

The most famous mummy is King Tut. He was still a teenager when he died over 4,000 years ago. He was put into a secret tomb. Scientists found this tomb in 1922. His family had put all sorts of gold, gems, and other riches into his tomb. Inside, King Tut's mummy lay in a solid gold coffin. Even his sandals were made of pure gold.

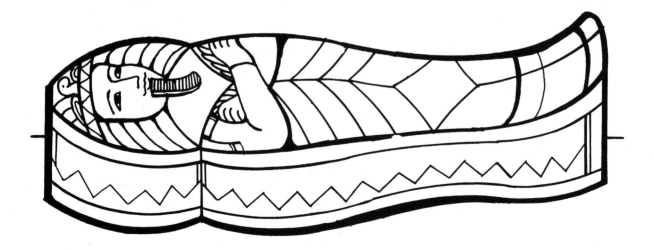

Mummies in Ancient Egypt

Comprehension Questions

Fill in the bubble next to the best answer. You may look back at the story.

1. **Ancient Egyptians believed dead kings and queens**
   - (a) would use their belongings after they died.
   - (b) should be burned instead of buried.
   - (c) would send good luck to their people.
   - (d) would return to their throne after they died.

2. **What did the priests do last when making a mummy?**
   - (a) They washed the body.
   - (b) They removed the organs.
   - (c) They wrapped the body.
   - (d) They stuffed the body.

3. **Egyptians mummified their rulers because**
   - (a) they thought it would make the rulers look better in the afterlife.
   - (b) they thought the rulers needed their bodies in the afterlife.
   - (c) they wanted to use the rulers' organs.
   - (d) they hoped the rulers would be found years later.

4. **The opposite of *preserved* is**
   - (a) kept.
   - (b) worshipped.
   - (c) ruined.
   - (d) changed.

5. **Today most people who believe in an afterlife call it**
   - (a) a funeral home.
   - (b) a graveyard.
   - (c) a pyramid.
   - (d) heaven.

6. **Picture discovering a mummy's tomb. What don't you see inside?**
   - (a) gold dishes
   - (b) a gold watch
   - (c) silver jewelry
   - (d) diamonds

7. **Do you think that mummy's tombs should be opened so that the world can see their treasures? Explain.**

   _____

   _____

   _____

History Standard: Understands the causes and nature of movements of large groups of people into and within the United States, now and long ago

Benchmark: Understands the various movements of large groups of people in the history of the U.S.

To Oregon or Bust!

Between 1800 and 1860 many people moved west. Farmers had heard of the rich soil and open land for animals to graze. The West also had supplies of gold, silver, coal, iron, copper, and timber.

The people usually followed trails that fur trappers or Native Americans had made. The Oregon Trail was one of the most well traveled. It went from Missouri to Oregon. It took about five months to travel its 2,000 miles. Some settlers followed the bumpy dirt path on horses. Others rode in wagons pulled by mules or oxen. These wagons had wooden boxes covered by a canvas tarp. The people packed bedding, guns, tools, and food in the wagons. To keep the weight down, they left behind anything that wasn't necessary. Still, when an animal died or got too weak to keep pulling the heavy wagon, they had to drop things beside the trail.

Families formed wagon trains. Each train had 30 to 70 wagons. The group hired a man as a guide and leader. Usually he had been a fur trapper who knew the trail well. Even in a big group, people faced **jeopardy** on the Oregon Trail. The settlers had to face heat, dust storms, and tornadoes. They entered a land that the Native Americans had lived in for thousands of years. Native Americans attacked the pioneers. So did thieves and wolves. Illnesses and a lack of medicine and proper food killed many people. Graves along the trail marked those who didn't make it.

The pioneers had to cross the Great Plains. Then they had to get through the Rocky Mountains before winter. Otherwise, they'd get stuck in the mountains. Snow would block the narrow passages. They could starve or freeze to death.

In spite of all of these hardships, thousands of people reached Oregon. Then they faced new challenges as they tried to build a life in the wilderness.

To Oregon or Bust!

Comprehension Questions

Fill in the bubble next to the best answer. You may look back at the story.

1. Each wagon train wanted to get beyond the Rocky Mountains before

(a) fall.   (c) spring.

(b) winter.   (d) summer.

2. What happened first?

(a) The group found a leader.

(b) The people loaded their wagons.

(c) The people followed the Oregon Trail.

(d) People got together who wanted to go west.

3. What caused so many people to travel west in the 1800s?

(a) Diamonds were found.

(b) Free cattle were given to anyone who went.

(c) There was lots of land for growing crops and livestock.

(d) The West was a place of great natural beauty.

4. *Jeopardy* means

(a) danger.   (c) games.

(b) sadness.   (d) noise.

5. If a family had to lighten their load along the Trail, what would they probably drop beside the path?

(a) guns.

(b) furniture.

(c) food.

(d) tools.

6. Picture yourself on the Oregon Trail long ago. What don't you see?

(a) fields of grass waving in the wind

(b) tall mountains

(c) wide rivers

(d) farms

7. What do you think was the biggest danger on the Oregon Trail? Explain.

_____

_____

_____

History Standard: Understands how democratic values came to be and how they have been exemplified by people, events, and symbols

Benchmark: Understands how people over the last 200 years have continued to struggle to bring to all groups in American society the liberties and equality promised in the basic principles of American democracy

The Quaker Who Shook Things Up

Susan B. Anthony was born into a Quaker family in 1820. Back then only Quakers believed in the **equality** of men and women. When she grew up, she found that most people did not feel that way. As an adult, she wanted to speak at a meeting. The men wouldn't let her just because she was a woman. She thought it was wrong that women could not vote. They could not own a house or land. Women could only do a few jobs. Anthony spent most of her life working for women's rights.

In 1851 Anthony met Elizabeth Cady Stanton. They became good friends. The two women wrote booklets to tell people about their cause. They also got people together to talk about women's rights. Anthony wanted women to get equal treatment. She talked about the right for women to own property. She said that girls needed a good education.

One day Anthony and Stanton set a goal: they decided that they must get women the right to vote. If this happened, other rights would follow. But for women to vote, the U.S. Constitution had to change. An amendment was needed. To try to make this happen, Anthony voted in the 1872 election. She was arrested. The judge fined her $100. She refused to pay. After a while, the charges were dropped.

Six years later Anthony and Stanton asked a senator to introduce a bill to let women vote. He put this bill forward every single year. Finally it passed in 1919. Neither Anthony nor Stanton lived long enough to see their goal come true. In 1920 the 19th Amendment gave women the right to vote. This happened 14 years after Anthony's death—yet it is called the Susan B. Anthony Amendment. Women can vote due to her efforts. And just as she had believed, more rights soon followed. Now laws state that women must be treated the same as men. No job or opportunity can be kept from them just because they're women.

The Quaker Who Shook Things Up

Comprehension Questions

Fill in the bubble next to the best answer. You may look back at the story.

1. **Susan B. Anthony was most interested in**
   - (a) cleaning up the environment.
   - (b) helping orphans find homes.
   - (c) getting more rights for females.
   - (d) getting a better job.

2. **What happened first?**
   - (a) A judge fined Anthony $100.
   - (b) Anthony became friends with Elizabeth Cady Stanton.
   - (c) Anthony voted in an election.
   - (d) The 19th Amendment passed.

3. **Who continued to work for women's right to vote after Anthony's death?**
   - (a) Elizabeth Cady Stanton
   - (b) Susan B. Anthony's sister
   - (c) Susan B. Anthony's mother
   - (d) a senator

4. ***Equality* means**
   - (a) education.
   - (b) different treatment.
   - (c) same treatment.
   - (d) ownership.

5. **How did having the chance to vote bring women even more rights?**
   - (a) Voting gave women a say in choosing the government leaders who made laws.
   - (b) Voting kept women out of jail.
   - (c) Voting made women have more money.
   - (d.) Voting gave women a better education.

6. **Picture Anthony's face when the judge fined her $100 for voting. What is the look on her face?**
   - (a) happy
   - (b) confused
   - (c) terrified
   - (d) determined

7. **Why do you think it took so many years for women to get the right to vote? Explain.**

   _____

   _____

   _____

History Standard: Understands major discoveries in science and technology, some of their social and economic effects, and the major scientists and inventors responsible for them

Benchmark: Understands the development in marine vessels constructed by people from ancient times until today

The Viking Ships

The Vikings were a group of people whose sailors explored the North Atlantic Ocean from 700 to 1100 A.D. They lived in the countries now called Denmark, Norway, and Sweden. Since they lived so close to the sea, they used water as their main way to get around.

Over the years, they became expert shipbuilders. They even came up with a new way to build ships that let them go farther by sea than any ships had gone before. How? Their ships were the first to have a *keel*. The keel was a long, narrow piece of wood attached beneath the ship. It helped to steer the boat. Even better, it kept the ship from rolling with each wave. This let the boat move faster. Because it could get places more rapidly, the ship could go much farther without stopping for new supplies of food and water.

The front of a Viking ship curved up into a wooden carving of a dragon's head. This let people identify a Viking ship while it was still far away. Out in the ocean the ships needed the wind to blow their huge wool sail. But on a river, people rowed the boat. Each ship had between 15 to 30 pairs of oars. If the boat was narrow, one man would work two oars. In wider ships, one man worked each oar.

The ships let the Vikings set up trade routes throughout Europe. They actually discovered North America about 500 years before Columbus did. They even set up a small settlement in what is now Canada, but it lasted only a few years. Viking ships carried settlers to Greenland, which is icy. They called it Greenland to get people to go there. They also brought people to Iceland. The **descendants** of the Vikings still live in both of these countries.

All Vikings were proud of their ships. When they died, many rich Viking men and women were buried in a ship! Included in the ship were the dead person's belongings, such as jewelry and weapons. The Vikings believed that the ships would give these people a safe journey to the land of the dead.

The Viking Ships

Comprehension Questions

Fill in the bubble next to the best answer. You may look back at the story.

1. **Where didn't the Vikings live?**
   - (a) in what is now Russia
   - (b) in what is now Norway
   - (c) in what is now Sweden
   - (d) in what is now Denmark

2. **What happened last?**
   - (a) The Vikings invented the keel.
   - (b) Columbus discovered North America.
   - (c) The Vikings went exploring at sea.
   - (d) The Vikings had a settlement in North America.

3. **Why did Vikings want to be buried inside of ships?**
   - (a) so they could be buried at sea
   - (b) to show off their riches
   - (c) to have a safe trip to the land of the dead
   - (d) to protect their graves from pirates

4. **You are a *descendant* of**
   - (a) your brother.
   - (b) your sister.
   - (c) your cousin.
   - (d) your grandmother.

5. **Why did the invention of the keel change shipbuilding forever?**
   - (a) A keel made it easier to control the ship.
   - (b) A keel made it impossible for a ship to sink.
   - (c) A keel made the ship much less expensive to build.
   - (d) A keel meant that no one ever had to row the ship.

6. **Picture standing on shore and looking at a ship far out at sea. How can you tell that it's a Viking ship?**
   - (a) by the ship's sails
   - (b) by the ship's front
   - (c) by the ship's oars
   - (d) by the ship's keel

7. **Should the Vikings get the credit for "finding" North America? Explain.**

   _____

   _____

   _____

History Standard: Understands how democratic values came to be and how they have been exemplified by people, events, and symbols

Benchmark: Understands the ways in which people in a variety of fields have advanced the cause of human rights, equality, and the common good

The Generous Doctor

How do fresh fruits and vegetables get from the field where they grow to the store where you buy them? **Migrant** farm workers pick many crops by hand. They pack the food into boxes. These boxes go to your store.

Migrant farm workers have a hard life. They move from place to place. They must go where the crops need picking. The more they pick, the more they earn. Whole families, including small children, work in the fields. Still, they earn so little that children often miss school to work with their parents. This is the only way to make ends meet. Due to the poor housing provided for them and the physical labor that they do, migrant workers often get sick. Sometimes they have serious illnesses. Yet they have no money for medical help. One migrant worker decided to change that. His name was Francisco Bravo.

Francisco Bravo was born in California in 1910. His family came from Mexico. The whole Bravo family worked as migrants. As a teen, Francisco worked every day after school to help his family. During the summers, they followed the harvests. After high school, Bravo went to college. To pay for it, he worked two jobs during the school year. He did migrant work in the summer. Then he won a scholarship to Stanford Medical School.

He earned his degree in 1936. He never forgot about the other migrant farm workers. He knew that most could not pay for health care, no matter how sick they got. So Bravo opened a free medical clinic in 1938. The Bravo Clinic in Los Angeles gave free care to any needy Mexican American. Later Dr. Bravo gave scholarships to migrant students who wanted to study medicine.

Dr. Bravo died in May 1990. Los Angeles wanted to honor him for his lifetime of helping others. That fall, the Bravo Medical Magnet High School opened. All of the teens who go there plan to work in medicine.

The Generous Doctor

Comprehension Questions

Fill in the bubble next to the best answer. You may look back at the story.

1. The founder of the Bravo Clinic died in

(a) 1910.

(b) 1936.

(c) 1938.

(d) 1990.

2. What happened first?

(a) Francisco Bravo went to medical school.

(b) Francisco Bravo worked as a migrant worker.

(c) Francisco Bravo helped students to go to college.

(d) Francisco Bravo worked at the Bravo Clinic.

3. What did Los Angeles do to honor Francisco Bravo?

(a) The city built a medical library named after him.

(b) The city started the Bravo Clinic to help migrant workers.

(c) The city began a scholarship fund for migrant students.

(d) The city named a high school after him.

4. A *migrant* is a person who

(a) moves from place to place.

(b) plans to become a doctor.

(c) never leaves home.

(d) owns a farm.

5. You can tell that most migrant farm workers

(a) become doctors.

(b) don't get a good education.

(c) have an easy life.

(d) have good medical care.

6. Picture migrant farm workers picking oranges in an orchard. What don't you see?

(a) people on stepladders

(b) trees covered with oranges

(c) people wearing new clothes

(d) crates of fruit

7. If you could do something to help others, what would you do? Why?

_____

_____

_____

History Standard: Understands major discoveries in science and technology, some of their social and economic effects, and the major scientists and inventors responsible for them

Benchmark: Knows technological developments to control water, wind, fire, and soil and to utilize natural resources in order to satisfy basic human needs

The Pipes that Changed America

Do you ever think about the pipes that bring water in and out of your home? Can you imagine life before plumbing? It was very different. Houses did not have sinks, showers, or toilets. Before building a home, you had to drill to find water for a well. After you'd built the well, you worked a pump or turned a crank to bring up the water. Every drop of water you used had to be carried into the house. If you wanted warm water for a bath, you heated it on the stove. Standing out in the rain was the only way to get a shower. When you needed a bathroom, you went to an outhouse.

Around 1860, rich people in Europe started putting plumbing into their homes. Yet it wasn't until the 1930s that most Americans had indoor plumbing. The plumbing system supplied clean water. Often it came from the same wells that people had once pumped by hand. Clean water came to the tub, shower, sinks, washer, and toilet. The plumbing system also had another set of pipes to take away used water.

Today, the clean water usually comes from rivers and lakes. First it goes through water treatment plants. At these plants people add chemicals to **purify** the water. The clean water flows through big pipes under the streets. Each house on the street connects to this big pipe. However, out in the country some homes still get water from their own wells.

Waste water from sinks, tubs, and toilets leaves through sewage pipes. To prevent clogs, sewage pipes are wider than the clean water pipes. Since the 1970s more and more areas have sewage that flows through underground pipes to a treatment plant. After the treatment plant gets rid of bacteria, the water goes into a river or lake.

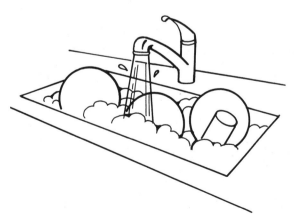

Indoor plumbing helped people stay healthy. They could keep themselves and their homes cleaner than ever before. Indoor plumbing saved time. People no longer had to run outside to wash their hands or get a drink of water. Plumbing also helped farmers. They could use hoses and sprinklers to help their crops.

© Teacher Created Resources, Inc.

The Pipes that Changed America

Comprehension Questions

Fill in the bubble next to the best answer. You may look back at the story.

1. **According to the passage, when did people begin to use indoor plumbing?**
   - (a) in the 1930s
   - (b) in the 1960s
   - (c) in the 1970s
   - (d) in the 1860s

2. **Which came first?**
   - (a) wells
   - (b) clean water pipes
   - (c) sewage pipes
   - (d) water treatment plants

3. **Why are clean water pipes narrower than sewage pipes?**
   - (a) because people don't need very much clean water
   - (b) because clean water never contains solids
   - (c) because clean water pipes are made of plastic
   - (d) because clean water is heavier than sewage

4. **The word *purify* means**
   - (a) to pollute.
   - (b) to flush.
   - (c) to clean.
   - (d) to evaporate.

5. **Why was it 80 years before most Americans got plumbing?**
   - (a) because it cost a lot of money to install indoor plumbing
   - (b) because nobody wanted to give up their outhouses
   - (c) because the inventor refused to share the technology
   - (d) because Americans didn't know how to pump water

6. **Visualize a bathroom. What does not use plumbing?**
   - (a) the shower
   - (b) the sink
   - (c) the toilet
   - (d) the light

7. **Do you think plumbing encouraged people to use more or less water than before? Explain.**

   _____

   _____

   _____

Answer Key

Note: Accept well supported answers for all essay questions.

Page 9	Page 19	Page 29	Page 39
1. a	1. d	1. a	1. b
2. c	2. c	2. b	2. d
3. b	3. c	3. d	3. c
4. b	4. d	4. c	4. a
5. a	5. a	5. d	5. b
6. d	6. b	6. b	6. d

Page 11	Page 21	Page 31	Page 41
1. b	1. d	1. b	1. c
2. c	2. b	2. a	2. b
3. d	3. a	3. c	3. d
4. a	4. c	4. b	4. c
5. b	5. a	5. c	5. a
6. d	6. c	6. d	6. d

Page 13	Page 23	Page 33	Page 43
1. a	1. b	1. a	1. a
2. d	2. c	2. c	2. b
3. b	3. a	3. d	3. c
4. d	4. d	4. b	4. d
5. c	5. c	5. b	5. a
6. a	6. a	6. d	6. b

Page 15	Page 25	Page 35	Page 45
1. d	1. d	1. c	1. d
2. c	2. a	2. b	2. b
3. b	3. c	3. a	3. d
4. a	4. a	4. d	4. a
5. b	5. d	5. c	5. b
6. c	6. b	6. b	6. c

Page 17	Page 27	Page 37	Page 47
1. c	1. d	1. a	1. d
2. a	2. b	2. c	2. a
3. b	3. a	3. b	3. b
4. c	4. c	4. c	4. c
5. a	5. d	5. d	5. a
6. d	6. a	6. b	6. d